ALSO BY GEOFFREY O'BRIEN

POETRY

A Book of Maps
The Hudson Mystery
Floating City: Selected Poems 1978-1995
A View of Buildings and Water
Red Sky Café
Early Autumn
In a Mist
The Blue Hill

PROSE

Hardboiled America
Dream Time: Chapters from the Sixties
The Phantom Empire
The Times Square Story
Bardic Deadlines: Reviewing Poetry 1984-1995
The Browser's Ecstasy
Castaways of the Image Planet
Sonata for Jukebox
The Fall of the House of Walworth
Stolen Glimpses, Captive Shadows: Writings on Film 2002-2012
Where Did Poetry Come From: Some Early Encounters

WHO GOES THERE

GEOFFREY O'BRIEN

DOS MADRES

2020

DOS MADRES PRESS INC.

P.O. Box 294, Loveland, Ohio 45140

www.dosmadres.com   editor@dosmadres.com

Dos Madres is dedicated to the belief that the small press is essential to the vitality of contemporary literature as a carrier of the new voice, as well as the older, sometimes forgotten voices of the past. And in an ever more virtual world, to the creation of fine books pleasing to the eye and hand.

Dos Madres is named in honor of Vera Murphy and Libbie Hughes, the "Dos Madres" whose contributions have made this press possible.

Dos Madres Press, Inc. is an Ohio Not For Profit Corporation and a 501 (c) (3) qualified public charity. Contributions are tax deductible.

Executive Editor: Robert J. Murphy

Illustration & Book Design: Elizabeth H. Murphy
www.illusionstudios.net

Typeset in Adobe Garamond Pro & Warnock Pro
ISBN 978-1-948017-98-5
Library of Congress Control Number: 2020942963

ACKNOWLEDGEMENTS

Some of these poems appeared originally in
Battersea Review, Marsh Hawk Review, Bowery Gothic,
and *Art & Letters.*

For Albert Mobilio

TABLE OF CONTENTS

WHO GOES THERE

From the start
there has been the question
of who may walk here,
whose graveled path is that,
whose locked storage shed,
from always
the stacked canisters of the fire station
have formed a wall,
in the woods the spent cartridges
have marked the trails of hunters,
and the lakefront has been guarded
by a fretwork of rope and docking
beyond which
altogether without paths or shelters
hidden under thickets
and never to be visited
the island across the water
may be stared at all morning without permission

NET

let them go
and where would that be

from the city
where trapped in conspiracy

of alibi and forced detour
they must submit false testimony

fearful of lost shopping carts
and unreported missed connections

failure to be in the right place
or to arrive when told

unable to get away
from being watched

in the entrance to the loading yard
or by glow of hall alarm

children condemned by night
to streets of secret wars

for whom the signal is not delivered
or the pass given

whisper and hide
among silent truck lanes

before there is enough light
for faces to be known

UN DESSEIN SI FUNESTE

"The passengers are not to know"
—not even suspect
that a play has been written
charting their activities in the days to come
hampering by stages their freedom of movement
as the ship changes course
and veers toward an archipelago
whose coordinates are familiar
only to the stranger who has not yet left his cabin

NEO-NOIR

In dream two subgenres
flourish with variations;

the one where you have committed a crime,
murdered a priest, say,
it may have happened years ago,
and now the machinery of investigation
has been aroused, or at the very least
the evidence that will convict you
can no longer be erased or concealed,
they are going to get you,
and in the illusory freedom
of finding yourself still at large
you are pierced by the terror of being called to account
and by unspeakable regret
at having done what cannot be undone,
even if it is never altogether clear
whether the regret is for the deed
or the misery of being caught;

and the other where the deed is not yet done,
the complex crime you have planned with confederates,
an incursion requiring timetables and cunning traps
and at the last a resort to violence,
a night watchman to be put out of action,
regrettably by lethal methods,
the set-up is a perfected machine
whose every detail has been worked out
over what seems like weeks of repetitive rehearsals,
except that as the trap is to be sprung

you become aware in one dizzying instant
of how dangerous and irrevocable
is the project you are engaged in,
horrible in its aims
and inexplicable in its motives,
and how likely a catastrophic outcome,
you are amazed not to have thought of this earlier,
yet giddy as you realize
there may yet be time to call the thing off,
you don't have to do it,
you don't have to take part,
you can walk away
and wake in the innocence
of having begun to forget everything

RUMOR PAINTED FULL OF TONGUES

"upon my tongues continual slanders ride"

There is no nice way to say this but we already decided
to stop listening to any of them, because they organized a conspiracy
against pillowcases and stitched aerials into our camping gear,
until even the shortest path to the machine shed
festers with toxic droppings. Where did the birds go.
Windowpanes have been banned. There will be no more ice treats.
Everything is a lie, even the word "lie", even the word "even".
In an emergency the first thing to fill out is a checklist
of missing items, trophies, parking spaces, weather alerts,
personalized keychains, things with your name written all over them.
Nobody wants you to know how long this has been going on.
(Hint: since before you had ears.) Your birthplace
had by then been farmed out to freelance coin collectors
and self-proclaimed fact-checkers. Barbarism has deep roots.
Neither civilizations nor planets are quite what they seem.
Money is in cages. Flat things are made to appear curved.
A hole is being dug right now under the street,
which is to say under the feet you have a right to stand on
in your own doorway, a right both unconditional
and under permanent siege. What looks like a harmless canopy
dangling over the entrance to a midtown high rise
is so often a signal visible to offshore interlopers
who are declaring in so many words you are incapable
of reading what is put in front of you. I didn't want to be the one
to say this but someone has to acknowledge that silence
can be deliberately manipulated. Think about caverns.
Think about locker rooms. Think about drinking fountains.
If that is too hard think about what is happening
in back of your head whenever you step outside.

It is not a picture anyone wants to look at
for any longer than it takes to recognize the fellow
at the rear of the subway car, the grizzled guy
with thick glasses and a neighborhood accent
who is about to tell you how things are
and you can already hear it in his eyes.

CLOWN HOUR

When the clown comes to mock us,
sent on his mission

in off-white face paint,
the smile glued in place

like a department store dummy
braided with joke explosives,

we mock him back to make him cry.
He strips us to our bones.

Art objects crumple in our hands
like abandoned wasp nests.

We did not expect death
during a comedy episode

or what would have been comedy
without the odor of ruin.

Nobody knows who sent him
or how to get rid of him.

Maybe the place is already empty
like a dressing room after the show ends,

lighting fixtures switched off
and unplugged wires tangled in coils.

On carnival night
everybody goes a little crazy.

Excited by what frightens them
and frightened by what excites them

the ticket holders advance with a certain urgency
toward the pavilions not yet on fire.

TWO TOWERS

As I emerged
from the Tower
in the basement of your Tower

(for there were found then
around the city
long rows of bins

whose red and green and yellow covers
gave promise of the unheard music
of Cameroon and Orkney)

being late I slipped
too fast through the gilded
revolving door of your lobby

and just managed
to get in the way of
the approaching figure

flanked by two bodyguards
taller even than you,
whose shoulders

as I obliged them
to break their rhythm
shifted unmistakably

into a defensive stance,
arching forward
ready to tackle—

cement men
made from the pavement
they claimed as their own—

in which same instant
I saw you
and knew you—

a stolid block
the face almost a golem's
the eyes keen

to dart
toward the point
of blockage

so as to grant me
the sense of what it is
to be looked at

as a bug is looked at
when startled by light
it scurries toward the wall—

or as a clumsy servant
who stumbles
in his patron's walkway—

not contempt but irritation
that even for a half-second
your stride should be interrupted—

your dignity offended—
until your eyes
having made the assessment

slid back
into their lair—
that Tower is gone,

that basement garden
where the hope of the new
sprang into blossom

at the bottom of the escalator—
I have dreamt of it
so often

with its rows of
undiscovered island music
and excavated operas

remote roadside jukebox playlists
danceband sessions from coastal bars
reconstructed soundtracks

madcap jazz transferred to shellac
in an occupied city
the last unaccompanied tapes laid down

in a barely furnished hotel room—
the place where the lost
was always being found again—

as I strain to imagine
what you in the meantime
were listening to through gilded ear-buds—

a compilation of oompah bands
perhaps, or the best of death metal,
or like your role model Charles Foster Kane

a song composed in your praise?
or merely a canned soundtrack
moving in vacant loops,

the sort allotted to everyone else
when the customer service line
puts them on hold,

the sound of the eternal
background that gives
nothing back?

That Tower is gone
and yours
stands fast

though ringed by armed agents
and concrete bollards—
and likewise on every channel

however fast
I click on past
the eyes maintain their surveillance

725 Fifth Avenue,
New York City December 2016
and in memory of Tower Records

ANCIENT WORLD

These to be remembered
Omens and prodigies
Prophetic dreams
Unearthly voices
Extraordinary luck
Extraordinary misfortune
Extraordinary cruelty
Extraordinary refinements of humiliation and insult
Extraordinary patience in exacting revenge
Extremes of pride
Extremes of wrath
Extremes of self-deception
Extremes of concealed cunning
The deepest mastery of the secrets of strategy
The deepest intuition of the secrets of nature
The surest judgment in utterance
Or more difficult yet in remaining silent
The drowning of a city
The disappearance of an army in the desert
The collapse of a kingdom
By reason of an oracle misread

MEROVINGIAN DAYS

That one
had big ideas
about controlling
the shipments of payments;

he lied his way
into the storeroom;
jiggered
the loading tally;

had a lot of friends
on both sides of the line
who never minded
doing a small favor;

on hot afternoons
in the shade of the granary
he thought about the odds
for making his meditated move;

but fate wanted him
taken down in a doorway,
stripped from the register
and buried without a name

SENDERO PERDIDO

To sweat it out in a room on the top floor
checking the roofs across the street for snipers,
that is no more than the common fate
of a washed-up bounty killer,
or a marshal at odds with a half-cracked range boss
whose hired guns have for weeks milled around
groping barmaids and hazing local merchants
while they wait for the go-ahead –

To be registering at four in the morning
that it didn't have to end in a boxed-up town
whose streets lead nowhere anymore
but to the abandoned mineshaft
where they used to dump bodies after the war,
or imagining how it would have been
if everybody hadn't silently agreed to forget
the night raids and the intercepted mail bags,

that would only be the dead-end canyon
where words head when the town runs dry
of names to whisper about and there is nothing left
in that sweet roost of a hilltop cabin
but a smashed lantern and a rusted coffee pot
at the end of a pathway overgrown with brambles
out where you shiver at the cry of a coyote
out there where the wind blows free

WILD HORSES

Would have been trampled
a hundred times over

if he hadn't made
a poem of them

galloping through the dark
among unseen hills

HOSPITALITY CENTER

—came back too late
after the coat check closed

and walked in the halls
of a different time zone—

even the lights
on the water switched off—

to shelter in the armchair
of a pitch dark lobby

THE COUNTERSIGN

the news came in the voice
of someone who escaped

skimming across the yard
like winter air

how fast does light travel
in rain

and when it comes down
all night

how many voices
glisten in the sound of it

THE FOG

Who are those people
over the hill

and who even said
it was a hill

and were they paid
to say so

Whose morning is it
that they would rather die

than admit
is going to outlive them

THEY CAME FROM BEYOND SPACE

We were told
that they would come
that they would hover
that they would infiltrate
that they would be indistinguishable
that they would set up checkpoints
that their eyes would be concealed by dark glasses
that their voices would be monotone in quality
that they would carry black attaché cases
that they would inhabit caves
that they would inhabit abandoned mineshafts
that they would take vegetable form
that they would take vaporous form
that they would take electromagnetic form
that they would organize the construction of giant
    habitable gas tanks
that they would seal off regions by invisible barriers
that they would commandeer brain functions
that they would enlist truck drivers and farm laborers
that they would enlist glibly articulate emissaries
that they would undermine chains of command
that they would instill mindless loyalty
that they would neutralize communications networks
that they would operate advanced weaponry by remote control
that they would broadcast simultaneous multilingual bulletins
that they would speak without words
that they would speak through the voices of the possessed
that they would employ mathematics as a language
that they would communicate among themselves
    by piercingly high-pitched music

that they would deploy with hivelike discipline
that they would level cities by way of example
that they would abduct women of childbearing age
that they would abduct molecular biologists
that they would perform inconceivably advanced neural
    surgery
that they would seek blood
that they would seek breathable air
that they would be ancient
that they would be indifferent
that they would be incapable of pity
that they would be acquainted with catastrophe
that they would be in flight from a depleted homeland
that they would be in despair
that they would be tortured by regret for what they had lost
that they would come as advance agents
that they would come again
that they would come in greater numbers
that they had already come
that they had never left
that they were us

VERTIGO

It closes in
on what it
draws away from—

a spiral contraption
that strictly speaking
goes nowhere—

yet its name
if it had one
would be "The Voyage"—

and if it had
a picture on its
curved wall

it would show
fruit on branches
bending down

and a stream
circling about
a splendid lawn

where a company
(gathered to murmur
words fashioned

into songlike structures
among whose vibrations
the very sky is braided)

calls and responds
in kind until the hour
has opened up

past the point
where it can ever again
be sealed—

and the name
of the picture
would be "The Arrival"

THE CANDLE

Far to the north
a single light
burns in the dark

by which to parse
the grammar
of a sentence

a sentence without meaning
but whose verb
so naggingly

fails to agree
in number
with its subject

(*it are*
it are
it are)

that against this lack
of agreement
the mind

in northern solitude
bangs up
again and again—

while to the south
all lands lie buried
in earthy silence

not even hearing
the breakers
smashing

without end
against their banks
to wear down

every last particle
of matter that yet
continues to resist

AT A GLANCE

the days not marked
on the calendar

the ones that ruin
the ones that came before

leaving only
premonition as comfort

NIGHT SONG

Through vale hall
the sea noise

bloweth forever
in utter darkness

—Just ask the lady
who stole the tape

so she could listen
without stirring

from her cabin
in the middle of the mountain

THE VISITOR

just past the fingertips
just where the voice stops

just above the skull dome
just behind the neck bone

just beyond eye range
just out of earshot

a bit too far to walk to
a bit too small to make out

much too wide to size up
much too loose to grab hold of

it has been hovering
for what seems like always

and has always
just zipped off

THE WHISPER

I saw
but could not tell you,

I almost
heard him say—

so hard
to be close

and feel it
close shut—

uninterrupted
sentence

begun in the dark
I can't know when

that ought to have been
roomy enough

for autumns
without end

and hours
without beginnings—

THE VIGIL

After so many years
it comes to this—

To be standing
by the open door

in an icy wind
at midnight

waiting for the absent mother
to emerge

as a mad ghost
from the surrounding dark—

She must be out there
somewhere roaming around—

As I stifle the urge
to call toward the shadows

as if to someone
late getting home—

NORTH FORD

for LaVerne Owens, in memory

To have been
only that

a vestibule
where voices gather
in a thrum of murmur

only to have
been that

—

The end of the end
of summer is to watch
the stars in the dark in silence

stretched out flat
for hours between constellations
and fireflies

words are there
to write down
nothing

in space
where none is
over or under any

—

If something should go wrong
with the sun

If the stars should drop
from their bright net

—

Our known world
a toy

in the fumbling grip
of an easily distracted

galactic
toddler

—

That they depart
is clear to see

but into what twin universe
could they have gone

—

We will be ghosts
walking in and out
of other people's dreams

—

In the ancient
world

the back porch
by setting sun

was a fine time
to joke

a nice time
to light up a smoke

to feel wooden boards
under the feet

–

A black horse alone on a road

–

You have to go
the long way around

if you want to get nowhere
on time

–

Bending down
for fallen crumbs

trying to sweep up
reflected light

—

Only a true-hearted atheist
could have shown such spirit

gay
in the old sense

the sound of your voice pure fun
no matter the words

—

Who taught me
it is only
a paper moon

—

At the very last
is it like

it's happening
to someone else

—

Once there was water
and it ran under the planks

Oh the soft gurgle
oh the silken trickle

–

If even two strangers
who happen to take shelter

from the rain
under the same tree

must have been connected
in another life

how much more then
we

–

A dream of missing letters
making spaces within words

every other sentence omitted forever

the remnants to be repeated
at intervals

wake up naked and with nothing

–

A note on the text

it survives
by being harmed

finally is almost only
its gashes and gaps

Glade Road, summer 2017

HORACIO SALGÁN

To go quick
ever so slowly

To go slow
quickly

To bounce off
what happens

Always
in the same place

Where quick notes
drip down like slow rain

SEQUESTRATION

What is there to work with
but the sound of other voices.
The later you come to a place
the more quickly it fills with absences.

In his late compendium
"The Decline of the Real"
he had written: "History has room
only for the inconceivable."

A nostalgia for the world.
The lotus pond
not yet drained.
The air they lived on.

What will you take
to the hills if you can get there,
if in the heat
they have not already lost their minds.

Fated even now to listen for Andromeda
pleading from a distant rock.
Mixed with the groans of the emaciated
from an unlit sub-basement.

A ghost rider crying for a wildflower.
Need some amino acid,
some glycine and phosphorus
or nothing will happen.

Violence is a language
like any other
except it only tells you
what you don't want to hear.

UNCERTAINTY

Never to have realized that he was her cousin,
or that the novella about the trip up the Amazon
was just a furtive way of talking about Dayton
and the questionable relations that once prevailed there
would be strictly an introductory level
of miscomprehension compared with not being aware
of how the apartment even came to be inhabited
and to what end, or what earlier episodes
of forced flight from unrecoverable addresses
had been obscured under layers of aliases,
just as the belated and disturbing revelation
that what sounded for all the world like a grackle
piercing the garden air at first light
was really a sort of dematerialized piano,
and that consequently the whole spectrum
of distinct auditory impressions was put in doubt,
could hardly be compared with no longer being quite sure
how many years had passed since that last glance
down into the street where an acquaintance
strode with vigorous youthful step
toward the metro entrance or whether that
was not another with another name
and perhaps in a different city, perhaps
not an acquaintance at all, if indeed
there had ever been acquaintances not dreamt
or conjured out of tricks of juxtaposition,
and in the exquisite disorder of that uncertainty
to hold up a hand to the light and say what *is* that,
how long has it been there, what is it called.

IN CITIES

In cities are neighborhoods not often seen
or that perhaps when seen are never remembered,
their streets joined by tunnels and crosswalks
that lose themselves in winding detours,
so that the friend you saw paused by a railing
only a dozen yards away (his eyes turned
toward the plaza below, and with whom you so urgently
needed to share a recollection that only in that instant
had come to mind, a message from someone
long absent that was like the news of an escape)
could not be approached directly but only
by moving out of sight into an unlit underpass
and proceeding yet further from the point you wanted to reach
along curved paths circling toward a remote inner portal.

FROM A LOST HYMNBOOK

he moveth like a river
within the nations

in music dwelleth
among chasms between chords

hath drawn fire upward
as from a well

and on water hath printed
the face of what never was seen

THE ASSAULT ON REASON BY DIVINE LOVE

It begins on the level of language, of letters even,
even if the letters are too small to read
and the closely set type barely allows room
for white space between the lines or anything at all
that would soften or sweeten or in any way moderate
the stark declaration of those serifs and slant bars,
those dread colophons announcing inevitable conclusions,
those periods heavy like leaden balls
marking the limits of sentences beyond appeal,
yet the paper is brittle, the binding tattered,
and the cover of the volume has half come loose
in the bin where it was tossed among random discards,
there is hardly a moment to hold it in the hand
without time or eyes to read beyond the title
on the spine where the author's name
has been rubbed almost entirely away,
it seems to be by Someone of Somewhere.

ADDRESS UNKNOWN

The real paradise
is the paradise known to be unreal
the cities never visited
the legendary straits
or sacred clearings
that turn out to be there
the same way they would have been
had every rendezvous
found its appointed corner
just as the sunlight landed on
the line of stone
along the edge of the harbor

TRACES OF LIFE ON MARS

They leave marks
in which after millennia can be discerned
cocoons and snail-tracks and the abrasions
of a violent cavalry; a drooping bloom;
mouths hanging open in hunger;
seashells laid out in a semicircle
for a game of chance; the interior of a bell
seen from below; domed enclosure
at clifftop; bared breasts in a bower
or arms lifted in emerging from sleep
to salute the light; cups shaped like wells;
rivers where rafts go through stone lips;
bees' nests in crevices; a helmeted courier
crouching for a jump; a bent form,
the knees drawn up, the dozing head
tilted to the side; the crowd of dancers
who imitate the movement of waves,
so mingled that the bodies
cannot be told one from another;
the stare of a horned beast;
the hollows beneath ledges
where they can dream of debris aprons,
pouches, cauldrons,
and people them with talking shadows.

TWINE

I ask a ghost
to fix my radio
because it won't
stop playing.

Not quiet enough yet
to hear a thing
beyond the refracted
ocean waves.

Their meter
like random noise,
the tune gone
entirely into gong tone.

A broken ripple
scraped in rock,
warped
like trees seen through ice.

Hardly possible that everything
can have turned to glass,
nothing in itself
but what passes through it.

While a tongue sounds out
a property in language
to be absconded with and diverted
toward private ends.

I didn't live
but I saw the movie version,
or was it just the title track,
Love Theme from Other Shades of Now.

And was that an odor of lilac
from the dressing room,
a barely detectable residue
of gift or forgiveness.

As in a city
where you go into the gardens
to get away from the air,
the city so rapidly replaced by another.

Almost as rapidly
as its people
by those who walk
where streets formerly were.

Who have forgotten
without even the excuse
of being of an age
to remember.

By now so riled
about almost everything
that what they dream of
they must be scared of.

Not all having a genius
for recalling what never happened
but a good number skilled
at forgetting what did.

Since what could be more fearful
than a memory
but the presentiment
of a further one.

A future memory
for which the contract
is not yet signed,
the ink still wet on its clauses.

While thoughts indifferent
to who is thinking them
twine around themselves
to flirt with their contraries.

Get up early enough
to catch them at their tricks
and wonder
where you have been all your life.

Always vulnerable
if not already destroyed,
what humiliation to have been
defeated by mere language.

Not even language but the phrase
not yet spoken, passionate talk
as rough sketch of further talk
for which there may be no occasion.

Only the alternative programming
of the fire in the night cave
to throw retrospective light
on what was sketched by day.

Continuous interweaving of pathways
like the after-image of an inviting glance
before it goes to be tossed
on the carpet of rags and bottles.

Out under the sun among the flies,
while twisted memories of ancient lyrics
barge through the glare
like tears in smoke haze.

Come from somewhere
go somewhere,
cannot identify somewhere
with greater precision.

You go
the same way
words go
but sooner.

RENOVATION

On the shore of the new city
courts and parks
have been sculpted out of landfill,
food stands and marinas
as yet untouched across the channel
from the glass mirage, and bicycle paths
connecting the new lives to their new homes,
from which has been scraped
whatever might still harbor
an odor of the drowned and burned,
of the lives written down
nowhere but on perishable surfaces.

COASTAL LANDMARK

To seek what is
in what was, what was
in what was not, history
in a tale of sunken gold
and sailors' bones, a ruined tower
on a deserted road
in view of the becalmed Caribbean,
episodes acted out in air
but not seen, lives adjacent
but not joined, impressions
not discussed until forgotten,
the wreckage of the beach
where in plain view the matter
of their lives dispersed
into level roar, hard confessions
blew away as if unheard,
glances drifted over
the ebbing tide line
distracted by the pattern of it,
by then not sure
even what dialect
they had been speaking
or for how long, or how far
any had gotten from earlier landings,
at that point where the texture of skin
or cracked shell or charred log
is more like biography
than any biography could be,
in the place where names come
to settle into their sleep,
in their form of seeking

DWELLERS

Almost unable
to imagine where they have always been

for whom in the dark
the silence takes the shape of voices

spread through a periphery of glimmers
as if a robe swept the edges of bushes

in the passage toward a ring
always already joined

a perpetual clearing away
of edgeless encroachment

into filigree of song pattern
and celestial fern cluster

unknown to themselves
they discriminate

among path endings and undersides
domes and causeways

petals curved
to form interior alphabets

a roadmap of weightlessness
coming between anything and anything

perched
between light and lightlessness

inhabitants
of the invisible forest

THOSE MORNINGS

when the water splashing
against the tiles in the shower stall

sounds unmistakably
like a distant bagpipe ensemble

blowing ritual music
on a cliff above a sea cove

and you lose yourself
in the scarcely audible changes

LAMENT FOR THE CITY

if it hadn't been for the breakdown
if it hadn't been for the war
if it hadn't been for the influx
if it hadn't been for the slaughter
if it hadn't been for the earthquake
if it hadn't been for the eruption
if it hadn't been for the pestilence
if it hadn't been for the famine
if it hadn't been for the rioters
if it hadn't been for the scavengers
if it hadn't been for the marauders
if it hadn't been for the enforcers
if it hadn't been for the drought
if it hadn't been for the flood
if it hadn't been for the fires
if it hadn't been for the cyclones
if it hadn't been for the gnats
if it hadn't been for the rats
if it hadn't been for the locusts
if it hadn't been for the termites
if the trees hadn't gone
if the desert hadn't come
if the fireflies had stayed
if the birds had sung

the music would have continued
to rise at dusk over rooftops,
the aromas of small feasts
to have spread through courtyards
and alleyways, the shadows

of returning householders
to have lingered by the fires
around which there was talk
of blessings and mishaps
and rumors and complaints,
the dances of marionettes
to have acted out legendary
stratagems and hilarious
comeuppances, the homebrewed
wine to have warmed
the regulars while they traded
extravagant challenges,
the old and the solitary
to have leaned over balconies
and relished the rhythms and echoes
of the loiterers, the cloaked lovers
to have whispered on the sidelines
so that none might overhear
where they went when the moon rose

ABOUT THE AUTHOR

 GEOFFREY O'BRIEN, born in New York City in 1948, has published eight collections of poetry, among them *Floating City* (1995), *A View of Buildings and Water* (2002), *Early Autumn* (2010), *In a Mist* (2013), and most recently *The Blue Hill* (2018). He is also the author of prose works including *Hardboiled America* (1981), *Dream Time: Chapters from the Sixties* (1988), *The Phantom Empire* (1993), *The Browser's Ecstasy* (2000), *Sonata for Jukebox* (2004), *The Fall of the House of Walworth* (2010), and *Where Did Poetry Come From* (2020). His writings on film, music, theater, and poetry have appeared frequently in *The New York Review of Books, Film Comment, BookForum,* and other publications. He worked as editor at The Library of America for 25 years, retiring as editor in chief in 2017. He lives in Brooklyn.

For the full Dos Madres Press catalog:
www.dosmadres.com